STEVEN PRESSFIELD'S

THE

WARRIOR

ETHOS:

ONE MARINE OFFICER'S
CRITIQUE & COUNTERPOINT

BY

EDWARD H. CARPENTER

STEVEN PRESSFIELD'S
THE WARRIOR ETHOS:

ONE MARINE OFFICER'S
CRITIQUE & COUNTERPOINT

EDWARD H. CARPENTER

2620 S. MARYLAND PKWY
SUITE 975
LAS VEGAS, NV 89109

FIRST EDITION

ISBN: 978-0-9915572-0-2

ALSO BY EDWARD H. CARPENTER

HO B-52

LETHARGICA

SEVEN LIVES TO REPAY OUR COUNTRY

DISCLAIMER

The views expressed in this book are the author's own opinions, and do not represent the official position of the United States Marine Corps, the Department of Defense (DOD), or the Government of the United States.

As a man can drink water from any side of a full tank, so the skilled theologian can wrest from any scripture that which will serve his purpose.

– The Bhagavad-Gita

FOREWORD

Steven Pressfield begins his book with a note entitled "Writing About War," in which he states that he is a writer, and that this is what he does; write about war.

I am something a bit different. I too am a writer, and I do often write about war, but I am also a warrior; I have been for over 20 years, and I wrote this book in a war zone.

The Commandant of the Marine Corps publishes, on a regular basis, a reading list. It is designed to ensure that every Marine, at every rank, in every specialty is developing a depth and breadth of knowledge beyond that which they might absorb from their leaders or comrades, or intuit on their own. In short, this reading list is meant to develop what the Commandant has called "The 30 Year Old Body and the 5000 Year Old Mind."

I came across Pressfield's recent book, *The Warrior Ethos*, on that reading list, where it appeared to have taken the place of a truly great book, Lieutenant General Victor "Brute" Krulak's *First to Fight: An Inside View of the U.S. Marine Corps*.

I was looking forward to reading this new addition, as I'd enjoyed several of Pressfield's historical novels before, but was shocked by what I discovered; a rambling mixture of Laconophiliac hero worship, Eastern mysticism, and pop psychology.

As a leader and an officer, I was so concerned by the disturbingly misogynistic and backwards-looking nature of this book that I found myself obliged to write a critique to explain the book's glaring deficiencies, but soon realized that such a critique would only be half of what was needed.

Pressfield wrote his book in an attempt that was as well-intentioned as its outcome was mistaken; to define and promulgate a "Warrior Ethos" to help guide young (presumably American) fighting men and women along the path to success.

This book has been written to accomplish the exact same purpose; but I propose a much different moral compass than the honor-bound, shame-based relic of dead cultures that Pressfield has offered up.

To do so, I use a two-pronged approach. Just as recruits are broken down in Boot Camp, a degree of their individuality and civilian natures stripped away before they are rebuilt as Marines, so the first part of this book consists of breaking down Pressfield's concept of the Warrior Ethos, chapter by chapter, in a critique intended to show the reader the hollowness of the code that Pressfield proposes to guide us as warriors.

Then, I take the original, useful idea, and show how it can be achieved by using a set of thought processes and methodologies more in tune with the 21st Century AD than with the 4th Century BC.

AUTHOR'S NOTE

I am a Marine officer, and the book which I am critiquing appeared high on the professional reading list put forth by the Commandant of the Marine Corps.

Thus, in the course of this text, I will make frequent references to Marines, but where I do so, you could as easily substitute Soldiers, NATO troops, etc. In fact, any modern, traditional Westernized military organization should fit interchangeably with my use of the title Marines.

The principles I recommend would also serve a non-traditional, non-Western force, and are not inimical to an insurgent, guerrilla, or partisan military organization; in fact their adoption by such organizations would make their operations more palatable to the world audience, and allow them to better wage a "just war", even against stronger opponents.

As noted in the disclaimer, this book represents my own views, and is not the official position of the U.S. Marine Corps, the DOD, or the United States government.

PART I

THE WARRIOR ETHOS: A CRITIQUE

Steven Pressfield opens his treatise on the Warrior Ethos by illustrating the importance of women in a warrior society with a description of a scene from his earlier work of fiction, *Gates of Fire*. Pressfield admits the scene is completely fictional, yet he uses it as proof of an assumption that a certain Warrior Ethos is not "a manifestation only of male aggression or of the masculine will to dominance. Its foundation is society-wide."

In this opening salvo are exposed the roots of the several problems with Pressfield's entire thesis; his attempt to lay out a new guide for modern military personnel on the basis of a fiction that cherry-picks its facts from the historical reality, and largely ignores the true underlying societal issues in both the ancient and modern worlds while simultaneously claiming that it is society which must form the basis for the Warrior Ethos.

Let's look at the historical facts of the departure of King Leonidas and his 300 Spartans and compare it to Pressfield's fiction, where it is suggested that Leonidas chose the men as follows:

> Leonidas picked the men he did, he explains, not for their warrior prowess as individuals or collectively. He could as easily have selected 300 others, or twenty groups of 300 others, and they all would have fought bravely and to the death. That was what Spartans were raised to do. Such an act was the apex, to them, of warrior honor.
>
> But the king didn't pick his 300 champions for that quality. He picked them instead, he says, for the courage of their women. He chose these specific warriors for the strength of their wives and mothers to bear up under their loss.
>
> Leonidas knew that to defend Thermopylae was certain death. No force could stand against the overwhelming numbers of the Persian invaders. Leonidas also knew that ultimate victory would be brought about (if indeed it could be brought about) in subsequent battles, fought not by this initial band of defenders but by the united armies of the Greek city-states in the coming months and years.
>
> What would inspire these latter warriors? What would steel their will to resist—and prevent them from offering the tokens of surrender that the Persian king Xerxes demanded of them?
>
> Leonidas knew that the 300 Spartans would die. The bigger question was, how would Sparta herself react to their deaths? If Sparta fell apart, all of Greece would collapse with her.

But who would the Spartans themselves look to in the decisive hour? They would look to the women—to the wives and mothers of the fallen.

If these women gave way, if they fell to weeping and despair, then all the women of Sparta would give way too. Sparta herself would buckle and, with her, all of Greece.

But the Spartan women didn't break, and they didn't give way. The year after Thermopylae, the Greek fleet and army threw back the Persian multitudes at Salamis and Plataea. The West survived then, in no small measure because of her women.

Now let's look at the reality. First off, the account of Herodotus from which Pressfield routinely pulls his anecdotes tells a much different story.

Leonidas had come to be king of Sparta quite unexpectedly. Having two elder brothers, Cleomenes and Dorieus, he had no thought of ever mounting the throne.

However, when Cleomenes died without male offspring, as Dorieus was likewise deceased, having perished in Sicily, the crown fell to Leonidas, who was older than Cleombrotus, the youngest of the sons of Anaxandridas, and, moreover, was married to the daughter of Cleomenes.

He had now come to Thermopylae, accompanied by the three hundred men which the law assigned him, whom he had himself

3

> chosen from among the citizens, and who were
> all of them fathers with sons living.

Leonidas didn't choose men with strong wives, he chose men with living sons, so that if they were killed, their patrilineal family line would continue. So much for the fiction on which Pressfield bases his tear-jerking tale.

Then there's the fact that it wasn't really just 300 Spartans who faced down the Persian army at Thermopylae, but a joint force consisting of between 5000-8000 Greeks from Tegea, Mantinea, Arcadia, Phlius, Mycenae, Corinth, Thespiae, Thebes, Phocia and Locria – Leonidas' hand-picked troops represented only between four percent and six percent of the Greek forces.

None of the other warriors (over 90 percent of the total force) had been picked for the peculiar resilience of the women they had left behind, and yet miraculously, despite the loss of all the Thespians and many of the Thebans, Thespiae and Thebes did not collapse just because the wives, mothers, and sisters of the slain "fell to weeping and despair."

Furthermore, Leonidas did not "know the Spartans would die" when he led them to

Thermopylae; Herodotus tells us that the 300 Spartans and the other Greeks were only intended as a holding force, and that the Spartans:

> ...intended presently, when they had celebrated the Carneian festival, which was what now kept them at home, to leave a garrison in Sparta, and hasten in full force to join the army. The rest of the allies also intended to act similarly; for it happened that the Olympic festival fell exactly at this same period. None of them looked to see the contest at Thermopylae decided so speedily; wherefore they were content to send forward a mere advanced guard. Such accordingly were the intentions of the allies.

Moreover, the Greeks didn't have accurate knowledge of the true size of the Persian army until they saw it, and then held a council to decide whether to retreat to defend another narrow spot, or to hold at Thermopylae and send a call for reinforcements.

Pressfield is a great storyteller, but the morals of his stories, meant to be held up as exemplary to the current generation of warfighters are built on the flimsy fabric of imagination, not fact, and this will be a recurrent theme throughout this critique.

Finally, although Pressfield writes for a modern audience that is integrated by race and gender, he writes almost exclusively on the basis of Caucasian men of antiquity.

His Warrior Ethos, which supposedly consists of virtues capable of standing the test of time and informing a new generation, appear to have originated in ancient Greece, Macedonia, and Persia, and then somehow skipped over more than 2000 years of human history, lighting momentarily on the shoulders of the great Nazi strategist, Field Marshal Erwin Rommel.

Where are the Zulu warriors, the Mongols, the Vikings? Where are the Masai, the Red Army at Stalingrad, the Crusaders and their Muslim opponents? Where are the women, the children, the old men, and the slaves?

Although Pressfield has in fact written extensively about female warriors in his 2002 novel *The Last Amazon*, the exploits and abilities of women in *The Warrior Ethos* are confined to raising their children to be stoic, shaming them as boys and men if they show fear, remorse, or an unwillingness to kill, and bearing up without emotion when their husbands and offspring are ultimately killed at the convenience of the State.

That same stoicism served them well, too, when any of their newborn children who showed evidence of physical deformity were taken to the wilderness and abandoned to feed the wolves.

It is striking that, as I write this critique, we are currently in the "Month of the Military Child" and the Navy's Military Child of the Year, Alexander Ray Burch, was born premature and not expected to live through the night.

Apparently, his family was somewhat lacking in the Warrior Ethos as Pressfield imagines it – instead of exposing him to the elements and the animals on a rugged mountainside, they nurtured and cared for him, and despite his impaired hearing, they now have an extraordinary young man to show for their efforts.

THE WARRIOR ETHOS

So, what is this Warrior Ethos? Pressfield
believes it derives from the values developed to
allow small tribes of hunter-gatherers to
survive, values that are still seen in tribal
cultures in Afghanistan and elsewhere.

The Warrior Ethos, according to Pressfield,
consists of:

- Courage.
- Selflessness.
- Love of and loyalty to one's comrades.
- Patience.
- Self-command.
- The will to endure adversity.

These attributes, mastered and turned inward,
are believed to help a person control or
eliminate envy and greed, laziness, selfishness,
the capacity to lie and cheat and do harm to
our brothers.

Drilled into a person and turned outward, they
are also supposed to help us overcome fear and
the instinctive will to survive, and put
ourselves into situations where killing or being
killed are our sole options.

How is this done? How, in the span of a few formative months or years is several million years of evolutionary program overwritten with a new code? The tools that society uses, according to Pressfield, are shame, honor, and love.

Pressfield soon runs into a problem; his thesis is based on glorifying a set of principles that was generated in a historical epoch that he himself admits was "High Barbarism" and that lives on today principally in tribal groups and criminal organizations.

How to separate out the "good" Warriors from the "bad" ones, if they all embrace the same code, the very code he is advocating?

Pressfield ponders this point as follows:

> Every honorable convention has its shadow version, a pseudo or evil-twin manifestation in which noble principles are practiced—but in a "dark side" system that turns means and ends on their heads. The Mafia and criminal gangs live by rigorous and sophisticated codes of loyalty, discipline and honor. So do terrorist organizations. Does that make them warriors? Do these groups practice the Warrior Ethos? When is "honor" not honor?

It's an excellent question, and the answers are simple; yes, they're warriors, yes, they practice the Warrior Ethos, and honor is always honor, but only in the eyes of the beholder.

These answers should certainly give us pause – but Pressfield pushes forward, undeterred, and tries to differentiate the good Warriors from the bad Warriors by enumerating the similarities and differences between the two.

Incidentally, the fact that we're already making in-groups and out-groups and subjective value judgments about good and bad, right and wrong on page 16 is also a worrying sign of what's to come.

But let's hear Pressfield out on the nature of tribes - their social, cultural and political characteristics, because here he's really done a good job of summarizing these types of organizations.

> First, tribes are hostile to all outsiders. This has been true, anthropologists tell us, of virtually all tribes in all parts of the globe and in all eras of history. Tribes are perpetually at war with other tribes.
>
> Tribes practice the primacy of honor. Tribes are governed not by the rule of law but by a code of honor (*nang*, in Pashto).

Tribal codes mandate the obligation of revenge (*badal*). Any insult to honor must be avenged.

Tribes prize loyalty and cohesion. Tribes revere elders and the gods. Tribes resist change. Tribes suppress women. Tribes value the capacity to endure hardship.

Tribes are patient. Time means nothing in the tribal scheme. Tribes will wait out an invading enemy till he tires and goes home. "You've got the watches," say the Taliban, "but we've got the time."

Tribes are tied to the land and draw strength from the land. Tribes fight at their best in defense of home soil.

Tribes are adaptable; they will take on any shape or coloration temporarily, if it will help them survive in the long run. Tribes will ally with enemy tribes to repel the greater threat of an invader, then go back to killing one another once the invader has been driven out.

So far, so good. Pressfield and I are in complete agreement, but then he makes this jaw-dropping assertion.

There is much to admire in these qualities. In fact, a strong case could be made that what the U.S. military attempts to do in training its young men and women is to turn them into a tribe.

In fact, there is very little to admire in these qualities, especially for the modern, professional military.

We don't want Marines behaving in a hostile manner towards "outsiders", regardless of whether those outsiders are U.S. civilians, foreign nationals, or members of other U.S. or Coalition armed forces.

We don't want a Marine Corps governed, as in days of old, by concepts of honor that historically resulted in everything from fist-fights to duels to the death.

We don't want Marines seeking to revenge themselves or their friends, which leads directly to atrocities such as Haditha. We want the rule of law, not of eyes for eyes and teeth for teeth.

We don't want to resist change, we want to lead it, and we don't want to suppress women, we want more of them serving alongside their brothers and sisters in arms. We don't care what Gods our Marines worship, and we're an expeditionary force – we're not tied to the soil of our homeland.

Adaptability, patience, loyalty, the capacity to endure hardship, and a degree of respect for ones elders – that's about all the useful characteristics that can be extracted from the anthropology of tribalism.

But while Pressfield has already given his blessing to a litany of evils, let's see what it is that bad tribes do that good tribes don't, according to him.

> First, tribes exist for themselves alone. An outsider (unless he falls under the obligation of hospitality) is not considered a human being in the same sense that a tribal member is and is not protected by the same notions of fellow humanity. Tribes are the original us-versus-them social entity. When this aspect of the honor culture is grafted onto a criminal, political or extremist religious doctrine—read: Mafia, Aryan Brotherhood, al Qaeda - the easy next step is dehumanization and demonization of the enemy.
>
> The Warrior Ethos, on the contrary, mandates respect for the enemy. The foe is granted full honor as a fighting man and defender of his home soil and values. From Cyrus through Alexander to the Greeks and Romans and on down to Rommel and the Afrika Korps (with some notorious lapses, be it said), today's enemy was considered tomorrow's potential friend—and thus granted his full humanity.

Any student of military history would be obliged to call bullshit on this one. Modern militaries since World War One have traditionally dehumanized and demonized their opponents, especially when the enemy was of a different race.

Notable in American history is the nature of our treatment of "Nips" and "Gooks" in our Asiatic wars, and of the way that Soldiers and Marines in Iraq and Afghanistan have perverted the honorary title of "Hajji" (a Muslim who has completed the pilgrimage to Mecca) into a pejorative that is dispensed as liberally as the previous racial slurs against Japanese, Korean, and Vietnamese opponents.

Lieutenant Colonel Dave Grossman, USA puts it like this in his seminal text *On Killing*:

> ...the language of men at war is full of denial of the enormity of what they have done. Most soldiers do not "kill," instead the enemy was knocked over, wasted, greased, taken out, and mopped up. The enemy is hosed, zapped, probed, and fired on. The enemy's humanity is denied, and he becomes a strange beast called a Kraut, Jap, Reb, Yank, dink, slant, slope, or raghead. Even the weapons of war receive benign names—Puff the Magic Dragon, Walleye, TOW, Fat Boy, and Thin Man—and the killing weapon of the individual soldier becomes a piece or a hog, and a bullet becomes a round.

Pressfield likes to invoke Field Marshal Rommel and the *Afrika Korps* as practitioners of the Warrior Ethos – and it's true, Rommel did treat the British forces as potential friends – because under Nazi ideology, the English were considered a true Aryan people!

Hitler had actually hoped to ally himself with the Brits (whose royalty trace their lineage to the German House of Hanover) before beginning his wars against the *untermenschen* Slavic people of Russia and the Ukraine, and was in fact successful in signing treaties with England in 1933 and 1938.

Had Rommel been facing black American soldiers, Russians or Jewish troops, his treatment of them would no doubt have been much different.

Pressfield's second point is similarly incapable of holding up to rigorous analysis:

> Second, tribes are by definition limited in size (since social bonds are usually of blood or kinship) and thus feel vulnerable at all times to bigger or stronger rivals. Tribes live by the siege mentality. They see themselves as surrounded, outnumbered and ever in peril. Again, read: Mob, prison gang, al Qaeda.

Again, we only have to look to history for our answer; the world's largest contiguous Empire was created by a tribe and existed for 168 years. The Mongols conquered this territory with a force of over 120,000 warriors, and the Empire dissolved not because it was besieged by external forces, but because of eventual succession issues that resulted in it splitting into first four smaller Khanates which were later absorbed by another tribal warlord, Tamerlane, as he established the Timurid Empire which ruled for another 137 years and spawned yet a third major tribal dynasty in South Asia, the Mughal Empire.

Compare this to the accomplishments of Alexander the Great, the megalomaniacal Macedonian who Pressfield spends so many pages fawning over. Alexander's Empire was, at its height, one-quarter of the size of the Mongol Empire, and collapsed into civil war a mere 10 years after the death of its founder.

Further, he writes:

> The tribal mind-set thus has no trouble embracing the concept of asymmetrical warfare and pushing this to its limits, meaning terrorism and beyond. If the enemy is bigger, stronger and more technologically advanced than we are, says the Mob / gang / terrorist,

> then we are justified in using any and all
> methods to strike at him.

It is not just tribes that will push warfare, whether asymmetric, conventional or even nuclear to its limits. The United States remains the only country to have used not one, but two atomic bombs – not against enemy forces in the field, but against civilian cities, as part of a British and American strategy of carpet-bombing German and Japanese cities to, in the words of the British Air Staff, "provoke a state of terror by air attack."

The head of the British bomber forces, Sir Arthur "Bomber" Harris, stated unequivocally that the aim of the air war on Germany "should be unambiguously stated [as] the destruction of German cities, the killing of German workers, and the disruption of civilised life throughout Germany," and went on to clarify that:

> ... the destruction of houses, public utilities, transport and lives, the creation of a refugee problem on an unprecedented scale, and the breakdown of morale both at home and at the battle fronts by fear of extended and intensified bombing, are accepted and intended aims of our bombing policy. They are not by-products of attempts to hit factories.

In the Pacific, a similar campaign was carried out against the Japanese, on a scale that, when placed in context of the United States, horrified even its architects, General Curtis LeMay and the future Secretary of Defense, Robert McNamara, who recalled of LeMay:

> I was on the island of Guam in his command in March of 1945. In that single night, we burned to death 100,000 Japanese civilians in Tokyo: men, women, and children.

In the same interview, McNamara recounted:

> LeMay said, "If we'd lost the war, we'd all have been prosecuted as war criminals." And I think he's right. He, and I'd say I, were behaving as war criminals. LeMay recognized that what he was doing would be thought immoral if his side had lost. But what makes it immoral if you lose and not immoral if you win?

So, clearly, it is not only insurgents and terrorists that have a monopoly on the intent or ability to wage war based on the principles of terror and attacks against civilians.

Pressfield now combines these two untenable points to reach his conclusion on what sets the good tribes apart from the bad.

> Criminal and terrorist organizations practice tribe-like codes of honor, but they do not

practice the Warrior Ethos. They are "shadow tribes." They are not warriors. In the practice of terror, in fact, the terrorist organization uses the enemy's embrace of the Warrior Ethos against him. How? By violating the honorable tribal/warrior code in the most shocking and extreme manner—i.e., striking civilian targets, using women and children as human shields, etc.

The terrorist's aim is to so outrage and appall the sense of honor of the enemy that the enemy concludes, "These people are fiends and madmen," and decides either to yield to the terrorist's demands out of fear or to fight the terrorist by sinking to his moral level.

What would Leonidas think of waterboarding or extraordinary rendition? How would Cyrus the Great look upon the practice of suicide bombing or video beheadings on YouTube?

Greek and Persian generals didn't need to televise their beheadings on YouTube – those acts routinely occurred live in front of an audience of thousands; and sometimes many members of that audience knew that they were next.

And while it's true that there are no records of these leaders ordering anyone to be waterboarded, it may have been because they were busy carrying out other inhumane activities.

When the city of Tyre resisted Alexander's siege and refused to surrender, he spent 7 months to capture it, and then crucified 2000 of its inhabitants and sold the remaining 30,000 into slavery. A similar fate befell Thebes, where Alexander's forces slaughtered the men, enslaved the women and children, and then burned the city to the ground.

The ancient historian Diodorus Siculus recounts:

> All the city was pillaged. Everywhere boys and girls were dragged into captivity as they wailed piteously the names of their mothers.

Ignoring the historical facts, Pressfield, having in his own mind explained what sets the "bad tribes" (the Taliban and the Mafia) tribes apart from the "good tribes" (Ancient Greeks and Marines) now intends to tell us how the tribe binds its members together via a Warrior Ethos. Of course we've seen that his distinctions don't really hold up historically, but let's attempt to suspend our disbelief for a moment and plunge ahead.

A CRYING SHAME

Pressfield was a Marine reservist in the 1960s, and his fictional books have captivated the imaginations of many modern-day Marines, myself among them. Thus the fact that he can be so out of touch with the modern Marine Corps, and with modern militaries as a whole is all the more striking, for example, when he presumes to label the Marines as a "shame-based culture."

> In a shame-based culture, "face" is everything. All that matters is what the community believes of us. If we have committed murder but we can convince our fellows that we're innocent, we're home free. On the other hand, if the community believes evil of us—even if we're blameless—we have lost face and honor. Death has become preferable to life.
>
> A shame-based culture imposes its values from outside the individual, by the good or bad opinion of the group. The community imposes its code on its members by such acts as shunning and public shaming.
>
> The Japanese warrior culture of Bushido is shame-based; it compels those it deems cowards or traitors to commit ritual suicide. The tribal cultures of Pashtunistan are shame-based. The Marine Corps is shame-based. So were the Romans, Alexander's Macedonians and the ancient Spartans.

While the Corps of the past did indeed have a strong element of shame-based discipline, the Marine leadership of today endeavors to "praise in public, punish in private." Nor is it to be expected that in the case of a Marine who is simply clever at disguising his or her misdeeds that "saving face" would be well thought of.

The same can be said of the Army, the Air Force, and the Navy – times have changed since the dawn of civilization, and leadership practices have evolved since the 1960s.

We no longer tolerate racism, sexism, or bias against sexual preference as we did back then – we don't haze our junior troops, or employ mockery as Pressfield's go-to examples, the Spartans, were fond of doing. It's ineffective, unpleasant, bad for unit cohesion, and against the law. So much for shame as a basis for modern military culture.

In Sparta of old, we are told that boys started their training for war at the age of seven, and this training lasted until they were eighteen. Stealing was considered a virtue, but to be caught would earn a boy a whipping that might result in death.

Remember, this is the Warrior Ethos our elder Spartans are displaying and developing – beating a child to death while the young man suffers silently, brainwashed by his society to the point that he would rather die than cry out.

And that, believe it or not, was the lighter side of Spartan training. Pressfield, though he must surely know enough of Spartan lore to be well aware of it, does not share the darker side – the institution known as *krypteia*.

According to Plutarch:

> Periodically the overseers of the young men would dispatch into the countryside in different directions the ones who appeared to be particularly intelligent; they were equipped with daggers and basic rations, but nothing else. By day they would disperse to obscure parts in order to hide and rest. At night they made their way to roads and murdered any helot whom they caught. Frequently, too, they made their way through the fields, killing the helots who stood out for their physique and strength...Aristotle makes the further notable point that immediately upon taking office the ephors would declare war on the helots, so that they could be killed without pollution...

Who were these *helots* that the young Spartan warriors were murdering in the dark? They were, simply put, another element of the

Spartan society of ethical warriors that Pressfield has chosen to ignore. Why *could* Spartan men from the age of seven to eighteen devote themselves to training for war, and then spend their adult life from 20 to 60 training for or fighting in wars?

Simply put, it was because early in the rise of Sparta, they had subdued the neighboring Messenians, who were then forced, for the next three centuries, to labor as serfs known as *helots*.

Functionally slaves, they farmed the lands of the Spartan citizens, and gave their landowner a lion's share of the grain, grapes, olive oil, and other products that resulted, allowing him to feed his family, pay to send his sons through military training, and devote himself to preparing for war.

All warrior cultures start with a great man, says Pressfield, and in ancient Sparta, that man was Lycurgus.

> Lycurgus outlawed all occupations except warrior. He decreed that no name could be inscribed on a tombstone except that of a woman who died in childbirth or a man killed on the battlefield. A Spartan entered the army at eighteen and remained in service till he was

sixty; he regarded all other occupations as unfitting for a man.

It was easy for Lycurgus to make such a decree; he wasn't obliged to work for his bread. And the society engineered by this "great man" which Pressfield uses as his model for soldierly virtues was one based economically on indentured servitude and slavery, where child abuse, a crude but effective eugenics program, and ritualized theft and murder were the order of the day.

How far would any member of today's military get who suggested that all occupations beside war are unfitting for men? And what does this say about the women who serve beside us? Lycurgus would have them home by the hearth. If America, or even just her military, is to be a warrior culture as Pressfield's book suggests we should be, who will be our great man? Where is the modern Lycurgus?

There is nothing wrong with acknowledging the place that shame has traditionally played in military organizations; but to exult it and suggest it should be a foundation for our current or future Warrior Ethos is, in itself, a crying shame.

RITUAL INITIATION, VICTORY & PRAYER

Pressfield is a great fan of the idea of ritual initiation – his ideal soldiers speak alike, wear their hair alike, suffer alike and achieve victory alike.

In the real world, Soldiers, Sailors, and Marines speak with various accents, in service-specific and unit-specific jargon, wear their hair in many different ways, and when they suffer, either physical or mental trauma, it is usually alone. As for achieving victory, the simple fact is that America has only achieved a single true victory since the end of World War Two; the Korean War was fought to a stalemate and Vietnam was won by the Communists.

Operation DESERT STORM, a just war fought with limited aims under the Powell Doctrine stands out as the sole bright spot, followed by a debacle in Somalia, failure to launch in Rwanda, a too-late intervention in Bosnia and twin campaigns in Iraq and Afghanistan that are unlikely to go down in the win columns, despite the cheery proclamations made from the decks of aircraft carriers.

Pressfield thinks he knows how the Soldier's Prayer goes on the eve of battle – but as presumptuous as it is that he who has never, to the best of my knowledge, prayed on the eve of battle should think to put words in the mouths of those who do, it's worse that he even makes use of the trite phrase "the eve of battle."

I sit writing this critique in Afghanistan on the eve of battle. I don't waste time in prayer. The fall of enemy rockets on a Forward Operating Base (FOB) is not something that can be influenced by invoking a higher power. It's a matter of statistical probability. Where they launch from, what angle, where they fall, am I (or that fellow Marine who I'm supposedly praying not to be unworthy of) standing at or near that spot?

In modern warfare, every evening is the eve of battle, and no evening is. We may be attacked, we may not. A patrol may go out uneventfully, or something terrible may happen. We are not huddled around campfires in a Grecian gorge knowing that somewhere out there is a Persian blade with our name on it. And 21 percent of the U.S. military is agnostic or atheist; not inclined much toward prayers of any sort.

SELFLESSNESS

The group comes before the individual. This tenet is central to the Warrior Ethos, according to Pressfield. And it's a noble sentiment, when in fact there is any truth to it.

Take the case of Alexander the Great, the Macedonian warlord who runs a close second to King Leonidas in Pressfield's pantheon of role-models. He gives us the example of a supposedly selfless act by Alexander:

> When he was getting ready to march out from Macedonia to commence his assault on the Persian Empire, he called the entire army together, officers and men, for a great festival at a place called Dium on the Magnesian coast.
>
> When all the army had assembled, Alexander began giving away everything he owned. To his generals he gave great country estates (all properties of the crown); he gave timberlands to his colonels, fishing grounds, mining concessions and hunting preserves to his mid-rank officers. Every sergeant got a farm; even privates received cottages and pasturelands and cattle. By the climax of this extraordinary evening, his soldiers were begging their king to stop. "What," one of his friends asked, "will you keep for yourself?" "My hopes," said Alexander.
>
> Selflessness produces courage because it binds men together and proves to each individual that

he is not alone. The act of openhandedness evokes desire in the recipient to give back. Alexander's men knew, from their king's spectacular gestures of generosity, that the spoils of any victory they won would be shared with them too, and that their young commander would not hoard the bounty himself.

We, in our day, know from history that this was no calculated gesture or grandstanding stunt on Alexander's part. It sprung from the most authentic passions of his heart. He truly cared nothing for material things; he loved his men, and his heart was set on glory and the achievement of great things.

The "great thing" he set out to achieve was to cut a wandering path through the Middle East and Asia Minor enroute to India, picking fights with everyone he met along his way, leaving puppet governments in his wake, and all to little purpose – after his death in Babylon in 323 BC, the Empire he had conquered for a terrible toll in blood and plundered treasure soon disintegrated.

A realist will note two things from this passage – Alexander could easily give away things which he did not need – and more easily, knowing that the men he gave them to would, in all likelihood, not return. Less than half of them did – the rest, including Alexander himself, died abroad.

Moreover, while Alexander was undoubtedly a great tactician and general, he was also a murderer (he slew his friend Cleitus the Black in a drunken rage) used torture and summary execution, put thousands of captured men to the sword, crucified still more, and then sold their families into slavery, most famously after the battle of Tyre. And this was a man possessed of the Warrior Ethos? A model for today's military personnel? The rational thinker must find this proposition disturbing, to say the least.

The historical reality is that, while Pressfield tries to convince us of the love and respect which Alexander's so-called selflessness engendered, his men actually mutinied on two occasions, ultimately causing him to call off his planned invasion further into India and attempt to return home.

"FOLLOW ME!"

Another tenet of the Warrior Ethos, according to Pressfield, is that leaders should, well, lead. From the front. And again, it's a neat, if over-used mantra, which he's neither the first (nor will he likely be the last) to champion.

> In the historic clashes of the Granicus River, Issus and Gaugamela, Alexander the Great's order of battle ran like this: allied horse on the left, infantry phalanx in the center, "Silver Shields" to their right, then the elite Companion Cavalry. At the head of this 1600-man detachment rode Alexander himself, on his warhorse, Bucephalus, wearing a double-plumed helmet that could be seen by every man in the army. He led the charge in person and prided himself on being first to strike the enemy.
>
> This is the concept of leading by example. But it also embodies the ancient precept that killing the enemy is not honorable unless the warrior places himself equally in harm's way—and gives the enemy an equal chance to kill him.

That second paragraph ends on an interesting note, and one we'll return to, but let's consider this "concept of leading by example." If we embrace the Warrior Ethos, we will lead our subordinates from the front, in the style of

Alexander the Great and Field Marshal Rommel.

And if we are simple soldiers, we should expect to see our leaders out there at the forefront, their Warrior Ethos on display, and indeed, this was the pattern up until World War One.

Archaeologists recently unearthed the corpse of the English King Richard the Third, who was brutally slain during the Battle of Bosworth when he was unhorsed while trying to kill his challenger for the throne, Henry Tudor. According to Robert Woosnam-Savage, a curator of weapons at the Royal Armouries Museum in England, as quoted in *TIME Magazine*,

> Richard probably got within a few yards of Henry before his horse probably became stuck in marshy ground or was killed from underneath him. On foot, with foot soldiers closing in, the fight becomes a close infantry melee... At some point he loses his helmet and then the violent blows start raining down on the head, including a possible blow from a weapon like a halberd... which I think kills him.

The unfortunate King Richard was struck at least 8 times in the head with melee weapons as he led his troops from the front; his death marked the end of the War of the Roses.

It was exactly this sort of leadership that resulted in a veritable "Who's Who" of dead officers in the American Civil War – 124 Union and Confederate Generals were killed leading their men into battle. In fact, a Civil War general was 50 percent more likely to die in combat than a common soldier.

This lesson was not lost on high-ranking officers – 49 years later, World War One killed 908,000 British soldiers, but only 78 of those were Generals, which equates to an 8 percent casualty rate, as compared to the 35 percent rate for common soldiers. Look at the statistics for World War Two and each successive war since – the numbers of dead Generals dwindle to insignificance as they arrange to absent themselves from the front lines.

Junior officers in the Great War actually suffered the proportionally worst casualties of any rank, since they routinely exercised heroic leadership at the front of their men in the style of Alexander and Leonidas. But war had changed, and a willingness to lead from the front only meant an increased probability of dying young – the average life expectancy of a junior officer on the Western Front was just six weeks.

So, beyond the ranks of company-grade officers and non-commissioned officers (NCOs), modern leaders don't lead in the way that Pressfield's ancient heroes did. It is more accurate to say that they direct operations from the relative safety of command centers far from the brunt of the fighting - sometimes based in completely different countries from where the wars are occurring. This is hardly a "follow me" style of leadership, so what does it imply for Pressfield's theoretical Warrior Ethos, and what does it mean for the modern warrior whose place is, in theory, to follow?

THE JOYS OF MISERY?

Pressfield opines that Marines take joy in misery. We don't. In recruit and officer training, we endure the hardships necessary to earn the title of Marine, but we don't enjoy it. In wartime we endure the hardships necessary to accomplish the mission, but it's not because we like misery, it's because there's a job to be done.

We don't take pride in cold chow, crappy equipment, or high casualty rates. Historically all those conditions were forced upon us due to our unique position in the Armed Forces. I have written many awards and fitness reports – I have never exclaimed upon an officer's ability to get his men killed at a higher rate than the Army, or complimented a Sergeant on how decrepit his vehicles were.

Again, Pressfield spends too much time looking to the past, and not enough time looking forward. The modern Corps is not scrimping on equipment or chow, and is not pilfering from its fellow Joint or Coalition forces as Lieutenant General Victor "Brute" Krulak, USMC (Retired) wrote about in his outstanding monograph *First to Fight*.

Our collective honor is not offended to hear that the Army (or Air Force, Navy, or other member of the Coalition force) has been picked to perform some mission – to assign missions based on a concept like honor rather than a unit's military capabilities is about the most ridiculous thing imaginable.

Pressfield tells us that when the Spartans and their allies beat the Persians at Plataea,

> ...the spoils included the great pavilion tents of King Xerxes, along with the king's cooks, wine stewards and kitchen servants. For a joke, the Spartan king Pausanias ordered the Persian chefs to prepare a typical dinner, the kind they would make for the Persian king. Meanwhile, he had his own cooks whip up a standard Spartan meal.
>
> The Persian chefs produced a lavish banquet composed of multiple courses, served on golden plates and topped off by the most sumptuous cakes and delicacies. The Spartans' grub was barley bread and pig's-blood stew. When the Spartans saw the two meals side by side, they burst out laughing. "How far the Persians have traveled," declared Pausanias, "to rob us of our poverty!"

America is not impoverished, and neither is the modern Marine Corps. If the Spartans came to visit our chow hall here on Camp

Bastion, they'd find we eat better than the Persians.

Even when we're out in the field, our MRE's (Meal, Ready to Eat) are a far cry from barley bread and pigs-blood stew.

WHAT'S RIGHT ABOUT THIS BOOK

In every book, no matter how bad, one can find some useful nuggets of wisdom, as in this passage relating to modern day Afghanistan, called "Scythia" in ancient times:

> When Alexander was preparing to invade the Wild Lands of the Scythians in 333 B.C., a tribal delegation came to him and warned him, for his own good, to stay away. In the end—the Scyths told Alexander—you and your army will come to grief, as all other invaders have in the past (including our friend Cyrus the Great, who was killed north of Mazar-i-Sharif and whose body was never recovered). "You may defeat us," said the tribal elders, "but you will never defeat our poverty." What the Scythians meant was that they could endure greater adversity even than Alexander and his Macedonians.

What's interesting there is that the secret to winning in Afghanistan is right there. The general who can figure out how to beat poverty in Afghanistan may indeed succeed in making it a safe, peaceful, and prosperous land.

HONOR

Honor, Courage, Commitment. These are the "Core Values" of the U.S. Marine Corps, so it's hard to imagine anyone finding fault with Pressfield's assertion that this is an important part of the Warrior Ethos that we should develop within ourselves.

> If shame is the negative, honor is the positive. *Nang* in Pashto is honor; *nangwali* is the code of honor by which the Pashtun tribal warrior lives. Bushido is the samurai code. Every tattoo parlor adjacent to a U.S. Marine base has this in innumerable design variations: Death Before Dishonor.
>
> In warrior cultures—from the Sioux and the Comanche to the Zulu and the mountain Pashtun—honor is a man's most prized possession. Without it, life is not worth living.
>
> Honor, under tribal codes, is a collective imperative. If a man receives an insult to his honor, the offense is felt by all the males in his family. All are mutually bound to avenge the affront.

Honor – a man's most prized possession – without it, life is not worth living. Consider that sentence. Honor is a *man's* possession. Without it, you might as well be dead. If a *man* receives an insult, the honor is felt by his *male* relations – who are bound to vengeance.

Thus do we see women excluded and the misogyny of Pressfield's thesis reinforced, and so too are the ritual suicides of the *Bushido* code and the honor killings of *Pashtunwali* justified. This sort of honor is, quite literally, a dead-end philosophy, although adherence to it might, in part, explain the horrifying rise of suicides in the American military since 2001. Let your unit down? Fail a drug test? Cheat on your spouse? You might as well kill yourself.

As for "Death Before Dishonor", it's a cute slogan, but let's think about what it's really saying. In 2012, about 78,000 soldiers left the active Army. This included soldiers who retired or completed their terms of service. It also included about 6,700 soldiers who were separated for misconduct, and left with Other Than Honorable or Dishonorable discharges.

A literal interpretation of "Death Before Dishonor" would imply that those 6,700 soldiers should have killed themselves – preferably *before* doing whatever it was that got them kicked out!

The notion is as foolish as it is macabre, yet this is the sort of thing that a rigid adherence to honor codes results in – suicide to redeem one's personal failures was a hallmark of the Japanese *Bushido* code, and homicides to expiate the moral lapses of family members are common under Islamic honor codes.

How is this an idea of honor that should be revered instead of reviled? Yet reverence is exactly what Pressfield would have us feel for this archaic construct:

> The American brand of honor is inculcated on the football field, in the locker room and in the street. Back down to no one, avenge every insult, never show fear, never display weakness, play hurt.

Nonsense. That sort of honor is antithetical to modern military culture.

Back down to no one? It's fortunate that General Washington didn't practice that philosophy, instead willingly backing away repeatedly from decisive engagements with the superior British Army until he had secured the alliances and French reinforcements he needed to win.

Avenge every insult? Imagine the consequences if every Marine in a unit attempted to avenge themselves upon other Marines, other Joint or Coalition forces, or local civilians every time they felt insulted, let alone injured.

Never display weakness? So, we should keep the anger from the Post Traumatic Stress Disorder (PTSD) bottled up inside, not talk to the Chaplain, not seek medical help? None of these are a recipe for success. All are a recipe for disaster, both personal and professional.

> Honor is connected to many things, but one thing it's not connected to is happiness. In honor cultures, happiness as we think of it— "life, liberty and the pursuit of happiness"—is not a recognized good. Happiness in honor cultures is the possession of unsullied honor. Everything else is secondary.

With that sentence, Pressfield puts another nail in the coffin of his own argument – how should American fighting men and women embrace a concept that goes against the very fabric of our own Constitution? It's unimaginable. But Pressfield refuses to take his foot out of his mouth...

> In the West, pride and honor are anachronistic these days. The practitioners of honor are often

ridiculed in popular culture, like Jack
Nicholson's Marine colonel in *A Few Good
Men*: "You can't handle the truth!" Or Robert
Duvall in *Apocalypse Now*: "I love the smell of
napalm in the morning."

Once again, unable to find a real-life example,
Pressfield reaches into the world of Hollywood
fantasy and pulls out the fictitious Colonel
Nathan R. Jessup as evidence that
"practitioners of honor are often ridiculed in
popular culture."

Practitioner of honor? This fictional character
ordered the hazing of a Marine that resulted in
death, and then attempted to cover up the
incident by lying and pressuring others to do
the same, resulting in the suicide of a fellow
officer. Where is the honor in that?

But another of Pressfield's observations about
honor should give us pause –

> This is the concept of leading by example. But it
> also embodies the ancient precept that killing
> the enemy is not honorable unless the warrior
> places himself equally in harm's way—and gives
> the enemy an equal chance to kill him.

We touched on this earlier, on the section on
leadership by example, but it is the last
sentence that is most notable. In modern

warfare, we do not give the enemy a fair chance – in fact, with airstrikes, drone warfare, and snipers, we take ourselves further and further out of harm's way, even as we deal death from afar.

Conversely, our opponents have used their own distancing technique – remotely-detonated explosive devices allow them to kill without honor – though neither we nor they will admit to this apparently fatal flaw in our respective Warrior Ethos'.

THE WILL TO VICTORY

Pressfield then quotes General George S. Patton, who said "Americans play to win at all times. I wouldn't give a hoot in hell for a man who lost and laughed. That's why Americans have never lost a war and never will lose one."

Patton was wrong then, and history has compounded his incorrect statement; in 1945, America and her Allies *had* won the Second World War, but America did not win the War of 1812, which resulted in a negotiated settlement that left the contested territories in a *status quo ante bellum*, and the Confederate States had lost to the Union, at a shared cost of over 650,000 dead. America would go on to fight to a stalemate on the Korean Peninsula, and to lose in Vietnam.

In the modern age, on the modern battlefield, winning is not enough. The experience of Iraq and Afghanistan has reinforced the truth of Vietnamese Colonel Tu's reply to an American Colonel who observed that the North Vietnamese had never beaten the U.S. on the battlefield. Colonel Tu replied, "That may be so, but it is also irrelevant."

Warriors can win battles; they can no longer single-handedly create the conditions for a stable peace to follow.

DIE LAUGHING

We are advised by Pressfield to cultivate a terse, dry, and dark sort of humor to help us deflect fear and reinforce unity and cohesion. The Warrior Ethos, he tells us "dictates that the soldier make a joke of pain and laugh at adversity."

That may have been a good idea 2,400 years ago, for men facing a battle from which all or most would probably not return. But the modern warrior will, in all likelihood, return from battle, and go on to live a very long life, potentially carrying the burden of PTSD.

Gallows humor like the quotes Pressfield shares from Leonidas and his fellow Spartan, Dienekes, has a place, but not a significant enough one, it is hoped, to form the basis of a Warrior's Ethos. A good ethos should inform one's life – and frankly, there should not be too many times in either the military or the civilian world when this sort of Laconic wit is really going to be appropriate.

CASUALTIES OF WAR

Pressfield again starts off with a few bad assumptions -

> All of us know brothers and sisters who have fought with incredible courage on the battlefield, only to fall apart when they came home.
>
> Why? Is it easier to be a soldier than to be a civilian?

First off, no, we don't. Some of us know someone like that – many do not. And about 27 percent of all Marines and Soldiers have never deployed to a combat zone. The numbers are much higher for the Navy and Air Force.

This raises a key point – who are the "warriors" that Pressfield imagines should possess this Warrior Ethos? Are they only the Soldiers, Sailors, Marines and Airmen of whatever specialty who have deployed to a war zone? Are they only the 15 percent who serve in combat arms specialties? Or is every military member theoretically a warrior? The sales pitch for his book suggests that perhaps *everyone* is a warrior!

Pressfield's blurb on the back cover of his little book tends to indicate that he believes it to be the latter:

> We are all warriors. Each of us struggles every day to define and defend our sense of purpose and integrity, to justify our existence on the planet and to understand, if only within our own hearts, who we are and what we believe in.

That's a great advertisement for a self-help book, but it's a damned poor description of a warrior, in this Marine's opinion.

As for the question of whether it's easier to be a soldier than a civilian, well, this is better addressed a little farther along, after we've examined Pressfield's thoughts on the civilian world in general.

THE CIVILIAN WORLD

The Spartans, Romans, and Samurai of times past, and the Pashtun tribesmen that make up the core of the modern Taliban all share an advantage over Americans, according to Pressfield.

It's hard to imagine what this advantage might be, considering that the Roman Empire exists only in the history books, Sparta never advanced beyond being a city-state in Greece, and the Samurai tradition ended in a tragedy that engulfed all of Japanese society at the end of World War Two.

The Pashtun tribesmen have arguably done somewhat better; they are the world's leading exporter of raw heroin and have fought a couple of superpowers to a standstill, but other than that, they haven't contributed much to advancing the human condition.

Pressfield, though, gives them all credit for being "warrior cultures embedded within warrior societies" in contrast to the United States, where "the American military is a warrior culture embedded within a civilian society." This, he observes "is an interesting state—and one that produces curious effects."

First, the values of the warrior culture are not necessarily shared by the society at large. In fact, many of their values are opposites.

Civilian society prizes individual freedom. Each man and woman is at liberty to choose his or her own path, rise or fall, do whatever he or she wants, so long as it doesn't impinge on the liberty of others. The warrior culture, on the other hand, values cohesion and obedience. The soldier or sailor is not free to do whatever he wants. He serves; he is bound to perform his duty.

Civilian society rewards wealth and celebrity. Military culture prizes honor.

Aggression is valued in a warrior culture. In civilian life, you can go to jail for it.

A warrior culture trains for adversity. Luxury and ease are the goals advertised to the civilian world.

Sacrifice, particularly shared sacrifice, is considered an opportunity for honor in a warrior culture. A civilian politician doesn't dare utter the word.

Selflessness is a virtue in a warrior culture. Civilian society gives lip service to this, while frequently acting as selfishly as it possibly can. Is it healthy for a society to entrust its defense to one percent of its population, while the other 99 percent thanks its lucky stars that it doesn't have to do the dirty work?

Time to set Pressfield straight on a few points; first, modern military members value their freedoms highly, and are well aware of the degree to which we have chosen a career that circumscribes some of those freedoms. We are very conscious of how much we give up, things that the average American takes for granted.

When I arrived in Afghanistan, my Marines and I found we no longer would be allowed to drink or have sex (even if our spouse had deployed with us, which is, in the modern military, not unheard of – the unit we replaced had one of these star-crossed couples in it!) We would not be free to talk about much of what we heard and did.

Does that mean we did not value those lost freedoms? Nothing could be farther from the truth! We did our duty, but always looked forward to the day when the restrictions on our liberties were lifted.

Aggression is valued in both military and civilian culture, but only in very certain circumstances. Cage fighters, boxers, football players – they are all allowed and expected to channel their aggression in certain ways. But beware the athlete that breaks the arbitrary rules.

Mike Tyson was paid well to punch men in the face until they lost consciousness, but the minor act of biting an opponent's ear cost him his career. Similarly, the military condones the use of force under very restrictive rules of engagement, but aggression in general, shown to your peers, your subordinates, superiors, civilians or even enemy prisoners will get you sent to jail in the military probably even faster than in the civilian world.

And when Pressfield asks if it is "healthy for a society to entrust its defense to one percent of its population, while the other 99 percent thanks its lucky stars that it doesn't have to do the dirty work?" he again conveniently overlooks the fact that the elite Spartan warrior class upon which he bases the largest part of his Warrior Ethos themselves represented only 3% of Spartan society as a whole, the majority of which was comprised of the slave-like *helots* and the non-citizen free men known as *perioikoi*.

So, America is unhealthy because 99 percent of the population are not warriors, yet he bases his Warrior Ethos on a society where 97 percent of the population were not warriors. It just doesn't add up. But Pressfield continues:

In ancient Sparta and in the other cultures cited, a warrior culture (the army) existed within a warrior society (the community itself). No conflict existed between the two. Each supported and reinforced the other.

Remember the stories about the Spartan mothers? When the Three Hundred were chosen to march out and die at Thermopylae, there was weeping and wailing in the streets of Sparta—by the wives and mothers of the warriors who were not chosen. The wives of the Three Hundred walked about dry-eyed and proud.

In fact, the Spartans were often at war with their own society – besides the regular nighttime acts of terror and murder inflicted by young Spartan warriors during the *krypteia*, the Spartans were obliged to subdue a revolt by the downtrodden *helots* during 465 BC, and massacred at least 2000 more in 425 BC, according to Thucydides in *The Peloponnesian War*.

And the story of the Spartan mothers? Just that – a story, made up by Pressfield himself – none of the classical sources (Plutarch, Herodotus, or Thucydides) indicate that there is any truth to that tale. On one point alone in this chapter does Pressfield get it right -

The greatness of American society, like its Athenian progenitor, is that it is a civilian

society. Freedom and equality are the engines
that produce wealth, power, culture and art and
unleash the greatness of the human spirit.

If freedom and equality unleash the greatness
of the human spirit, what does it say that the
modern American military remains the last
bastion of a class-based society, where officers
are notionally "different" from their troops?

What does it say that those who defend
freedom as a whole are often subject to a more
restrictive set of laws than all other citizens?

These are the questions that we may wish to
explore if we are to imagine a Warrior Ethos
that looks forward into the future, and not
back into classical antiquity.

COMING HOME

Now Pressfield decides to show us what the Warrior Ethos can do for a military member who returns from deployment, and again, continues to talk about an alternate reality.

But what about us? What about the soldier or Marine who steps off the plane from overseas and finds himself in the scariest place he's seen in years:

Home.

Has everything he knows suddenly become useless? What skill set can he employ in the civilian world? The returning warrior faces a dilemma not unlike that of the convict released from prison. Has he been away so long that he can never come back? Is the world he knows so alien to the "real world" that he can never fit in again?

Who is he, if he's not a warrior?

The answer may not be as far away as he supposes.

The returning warrior may not realize it, but he has acquired an MBA in enduring adversity and a Ph.D. in resourcefulness, tenacity and the capacity for hard work.

First off, no one is deploying for years at a time; the average Marine deployment is six to twelve months, the Army, 12-15 months. Second, the world isn't alien – it's been there the whole deployment, connected by increasingly better internet and phone connections.

Who is he (or she), if not a warrior? Well, assuming they were warriors when they left, and are staying in the military, presumably they are still warriors? And as for adversity, again, we need to be careful about assuming that anyone's earned anything.

These days, the majority of the U.S. and Coalition forces in Afghanistan, for example, spend some or all of their time on large Main Operating Bases (MOBs) and FOBs– where they are all able to eat ice cream with every meal, sleep in air-conditioned shelters on real mattresses with real pillows, enjoy hot showers, access the internet, take college courses, watch movies, and practice salsa dancing and roller-skating when they're not "outside the wire" on missions or engaged in their normal 12-hour workdays on base.

An MBA in enduring adversity? Maybe an Associate's degree. Resourcefulness, tenacity, and a capacity for hard work? Some do develop that – some do not.

Be clear that this is not to impugn the hardships that combat troops (infantry, combat engineers, female engagement teams, etc.) deal with outside the wire, or in the most austere sites; but the reality is that the Tooth-to-Tail ratio in modern warfare is such that those Marines, Soldiers, Sailors and Airmen who actually spend significant time outside the wire represent only about one quarter of the total deployed force.

The remainder, in Headquarters, Life Support, or Logistics units, are generally to be found (more or less safely, depending on the frequency and effectiveness of rocket and suicide attacks) inside the wire, on the bases.

THE WAR INSIDE OURSELVES

Here Pressfield changes direction – he invokes one of the epic sagas of India, the *Bhagavad-Gita* to demonstrate that we should use our Warrior Ethos to fight our inner demons, instead of physical adversaries.

> The Bhagavad-Gita is the story of the great warrior Arjuna, who receives spiritual instruction from his charioteer, who happens to be Krishna—i.e., God in human form Krishna instructs Arjuna to slay his enemies without mercy. The warrior-god points across the battlefield to knights and archers and spearmen whom Arjuna knows personally and feels deep affection for—and commands him to kill them all. But here's the interesting part: The names of these enemy warriors, in Sanskrit, can be read two ways. They can be simply names. Or they can represent inner crimes or personal vices, such as greed, jealousy, selfishness, the capacity to play our friends false or to act without compassion toward those who love us. In other words, our warrior Arjuna is being instructed to slay the enemies inside himself.

That's a partial interpretation, but it leaves out a great deal. Arjuna requires this persuasion because, before the battle, he is gripped by a sense of the injustice and futility of what is about to happen, as shown in these verses from the *Bhagavad-Gita* which Pressfield does not share with his readers:

> My Lord! What happiness can come from the death of these sons of Dhritarashtra? We shall sin if we kill these desperate men.
>
> We are worthy of a nobler feat than to slaughter our relatives – the sons of Dhritarashtra; for, my Lord, how can we be happy if we kill our kinsmen?
>
> Although these men, blinded by greed, see no guilt in destroying their kin, or fighting against their friends,
>
> Should not we, whose eyes are open, who consider it to be wrong to annihilate our house, turn away from so great a crime?
>
> ...if, on the contrary, the sons of Dhritarashtra, with weapons in their hand, should slay me, unarmed and unresisting, surely that would be better for my welfare!"

Here is the philosophy of Jesus, Socrates and Ghandi at work – better to be the killed by a cruel and ignorant opponent, than to sink to their level and destroy them yourself.

But Krishna convinces Arjuna to fight the enemy nonetheless, employing the same mockery used by the Spartan women –

> Why give way to unmanliness? O thou who art
> the terror of thine enemies! Shake off such
> shameful effeminacy, make ready to act!

Note again the recurrent misogyny of the
source texts – it is shameful for a warrior to be
effeminate; how then, do we reconcile this
with the 10.6 percent of women now serving in
NATO military forces?

Krishna invokes another method as well to
convince Arjuna to give battle – all men die,
but their spirits do not, so there is no evil done
in killing the men who stand against him.
Moreover, it is better to fight than pursue a
non-violent course because:

> If killed, thou shalt attain Heaven; if victorious,
> enjoy the kingdom of earth.

This is, of course, the same sort of logic that
motivates suicide bombers. Later in the saga,
Krishna will explain what makes a man worthy
of God's grace:

> He to whom friend and foe are alike, who
> welcomes equally honour and dishonour, heat
> and cold, pleasure and pain, who is enamoured
> of nothing,
>
> Who is indifferent to praise and censure, who
> enjoys silence, who is contented with every fate,
> who has no fixed abode, who is steadfast in

mind, and filled with devotion, such a one is my beloved.

Again, Pressfield has invoked an interesting manuscript; one in which we are guided to believe that conflict is the best solution, that whether you live or die (or whether our enemies do) there is no reason to grieve for them, or fear for yourself, and that those beloved of God may choose to be honorable and dishonorable, and uncaring as to praise or censure, which appears to directly contradict the idea of a Warrior Ethos that puts the concept of honor at the forefront.

In the end, the *Bhagavad-Gita* culminates in a bloodbath – thousands are dead on either side, and only Arjuna, Krishna, and a handful of his followers survive the devastation. Pressfield ignores this result, but does admit that -

> Human history, anthropologists say, can be divided into three stages—savagery, barbarism and civilization. Warrior codes arose during the period known as High Barbarism. Many noble cultures fall under this category, from Native American tribes to Cyrus's Persians to the Greeks and Trojans made immortal in Homer's Iliad. The Warrior Ethos's origins are primitive. Its genesis lies in the eye-for-an-eye ethic of humanity's most ancient and primordial epochs.

Indeed it would appear so. Thus the Warrior Ethos as Pressfield describes it, and as it was practiced by the ancient Greeks, Persians, and Indians is completely unsuitable for the modern battlefield; it is even more unsuitable for contemporary society, and for the future of military and civil affairs.

Pressfield switches gears again, raising the question of why young men and women in free countries choose to serve in the military. His answer? They are seeking a "rite of passage."

> When we enlist in the Army or the Marine Corps, we're looking for a passage to manhood or womanhood. We have examined our lives in the civilian world and concluded, perhaps, that something's missing. Do we lack self-discipline? Self-confidence? Do we feel stuck? Are we heading in the right direction?
>
> We want action. We seek to test ourselves. We want friends—real friends, who will put themselves on the line for us—and we want to do the same for them. We're seeking some force that will hurl us out of our going-nowhere lives and into the real world, into genuine hazard and risk. We want to be part of something greater than ourselves, something we can be proud of.
>
> And we want to come out of the process as different (and better) people than we were when we went in. We want to be men, not boys. We want to be women, not girls.
>
> We want a rite of passage. We want to grow up.

And one way of growing up, says Pressfield, is to go to war, to make ourselves over into one of the great Jungian archetypes; The Warrior. Pressfield's summation is as follows:

Jung was a student of myths and legend and of the unconscious. He discovered and named the Collective Unconscious, meaning that part of the psyche that is common to all cultures in all eras and at all times.

The Collective Unconscious, Jung said, contains the stored wisdom of the human race, accumulated over thousands of generations.

The Collective Unconscious is the software we're born 'with. It's our package of instincts and preverbal knowledge. Within this package, Jung discovered what he called the archetypes.

Archetypes are the larger-than-life, mythic-scale personifications of the stages that we pass through as we mature. The youth, the lover, the wanderer, the joker, the king or queen, the wise man, the mystic. Legendary tales like that of King Arthur and the Knights of the Round Table are populated by archetypes. Movies are frill of archetypes. Even a deck of cards has archetypes: king, queen, joker, jack.

Archetypes serve the purpose of guiding us as we grow. A new archetype kicks in at each stage. It makes the new phase "feel right" and "seem natural."

One of the primary archetypes is the Warrior. The warrior archetype exists across all eras and nations and is virtually identical in every culture.

There's just one small problem – Jung didn't see the Warrior as being an archetype.

Instead, Jung saw the *Hero* as being one of the main male archetypal characters, along with the Wise Old Man, the Trickster, and Shadow (or Devil Figure). Female archetypal figures included the Mother and the Maiden.

It's a fool's errand to try to explain in a few short sentences the theories of Carl Gustav Jung, who wrote extensively over a long career, and mainly in German, but sufficient to say that Jung did not believe that his archetypes were, in fact, a way to classify people as one or the other; rather, he believe that we all have the basic archetypes, Shadow, Anima, Animus, and Self within us, and that we adopt specific aspects such as father/mother/child, hero/maiden/trickster at various times, with such secondary archetypes sometimes overlapping.

Pressfield latches on to another source to justify his idea; the early 90's New-Age Male pop psychology book *King, Warrior, Magician, Lover: Rediscovering the Archetypes of the Mature Masculine*. One of the authors, Robert L. Moore, is a psychoanalyst who has been heavily influenced by Jung's ideas; his co-author Douglas Gillette is a "mythologist, artist, and pastoral counselor, and is cofounder of the Institute for

World Spirituality." Moore and Gillette's contribution to Pressfield's core concept is to tell us that:

> ...the human individual matures from archetype to archetype. A boy, for instance, evolves sequentially through the youth, the wanderer, the lover, the warrior, through husband and father to teacher, king, sage and mystic.
>
> The warrior archetype clicks in like a biological clock sometime in the early to mid-teens. We join a gang, we try out for the football team, we hang with our homies, we drive fast, we take crazy chances, we seek adventure and hazard. That'll change later. When the husband/father archetype kicks in, we'll trade in our 500-horsepower Mustang and buy a Prius. But not yet.
>
> For now, the warrior archetype has seized us. Something inside us makes us want to jump out of airplanes and blow stuff up. Something makes us seek out mentors—tough old sergeants to put us through hell, to push us past our limits, to find out what we're capable of. And we seek out comrades in arms. Brothers who will get our backs and we'll get theirs, lifelong friends who are just as crazy as we are.

The flaws in this line of reasoning are many. A boy matures through the stage of "lover" before he becomes a warrior? Not likely. The majority of modern warriors sign up in their late teens – to imagine that they've not merely become, but evolved *beyond* being great lovers at that point is a bit of a stretch.

And again, repetitively, the masculine theme of Pressfield's ethos asserts itself. Boys evolve, join football teams, look for brothers-in-arms, and wait for the husband/father archetype to kick in. Really? How does this account for the 14 percent of the U.S. military that is *not* male? A percentage that is expected to grow in the future?

Another problem is apparent when you understand a little about the actual makeup of the modern military. A majority of service members (52 percent of enlisted personnel, 70 percent of officers) are married; about 40 percent of all service members have children. So, how can they have evolved *past* being warriors to being fathers, mothers, husbands and wives?

The pop psychology just doesn't cut it when confronted with the boots-on-the-ground truth shown by statistics.

UNANSWERED QUESTIONS

Pressfield began his book by posing the following questions:

> Does a fighting man require a flag or a cause to claim a code of honor? Or does a warrior ethos arise spontaneously, called forth by necessity and the needs of the human heart? Is honor coded into our genes? What does honor consist of—in an age when the concept seems almost abandoned by society at large, at least in the West?
>
> What is the Warrior Ethos? Where did it come from? What form does it take today?
>
> Do we fight by a code? If so, what is it?

Unfortunately, he hasn't actually clearly answered many of them by the time he reaches the end of his meandering soliloquy, but let's quickly review each one:

1. Does a fighting man require a flag or a cause to claim a code of honor? Or does a warrior ethos arise spontaneously, called forth by necessity and the needs of the human heart? Is honor coded into our genes?

Not according to Pressfield, who says that it needs to be instilled through the odd combination of shame and love for our fellow warriors.

2. What does honor consist of—in an age when the concept seems almost abandoned by society at large, at least in the West?

Quoting verbatim, Pressfield believes that American warriors should "back down to no one, avenge every insult, never show fear, never display weakness, play hurt." Hopefully there will prove to be some other brand of honor that we could adopt instead.

3. What is the Warrior Ethos? Where did it come from? What form does it take today?

Pressfield tells us that warrior cultures produce the eponymous ethos through the twin levers of honor and shame, but claims that pride and honor are anachronistic in the modern Western world, as well they should be, given that his exemplars are fictitious brutes plucked from Hollywood war movies.

4. Do we fight by a code? If so, what is it?

Pressfield never actually spells this out, but presumably it involves some amalgamation of honor, selflessness, leadership from the front, gallows humor, a love for one's fellow warriors, and a healthy dose of the fear of shame.

Pressfield ends his book by telling us that the hardest thing in the world is to be ourselves.

"Who are we?" he asks, rhetorically "Our family tells us, society tells us, laws and customs tell us." Even Pressfield himself is ready to tell you –

> The Warrior Archetype is not the be-all and end-all of life. It is only one identity, one stage on the path to maturity. But it is the greatest stage—and the most powerful. It is the foundation upon which all succeeding stages are built.

Let us be, says Pressfield,

> ...warriors of the heart, and enlist in our inner cause the virtues we have acquired through blood and sweat in the sphere of conflict— courage, patience, selflessness, loyalty, fidelity, self-command, respect for elders, love of our comrades (and of the enemy), perseverance, cheerfulness in adversity and a sense of humor, however terse or dark.

It's not bad advice, when you put it that way, summed up in one pithy sentence. Sort of like Mary Schmich's advice to wear sunscreen, which later achieved an iconic niche in pop culture when Baz Luhrmann mixed it as a spoken-word track on his 1999 hit single *Everybody's Free (To Wear Sunscreen)*.

But we must do better; if we are to promote a philosophy, an ethos for the modern warrior, the warrior of the future, it seems it should be based on a firmer foundation than a millennia-old tradition of patriarchal, tribal values embodied in the text by two kings, one allegedly suicidal, the other a megalomaniac; a foundation leavened strangely with a dash of Eastern metaphysics and a dose of Western psychoanalysis.

The second half of this book, the counterpoint, will propose another possible Warrior Ethos, one more suited for the present and the future than Pressfield's was even for the past – for where today are the Spartans, the Macedonians, the Persians? It seems their ethos failed to stand the test of time.

PART II

THE WARRIOR ETHOS: COUNTERPOINT

In making my counterpoint, I'd like to start by providing a better set of answers to Pressfield's original questions than he himself has offered; from there, I'll address some of the more problematic issues raised by the book in general, and close with my personal recommendation for a Warrior Ethos better fitted for the 21st Century AD than for the 4th Century BC.

Like Pressfield said in his opening pages, this book makes no claim to provide a final answer; indeed, I will argue, there is no timeless, definitive answer to Pressfield's core question – "What is the Warrior Ethos?" – the answer has changed and will change over time. These are just one Marine officer's thoughts and observations on the subject as it pertains to the current age, and perhaps the next few decades.

But before I can address Pressfield's questions, I need to ask and propose an answer to one of my own; in this day and age, who is a warrior? Pressfield's suggestion that "we are all warriors" rings so hollow that a better answer is needed, for it is rather key to the discussion ahead.

In days of old it was a fairly simple question; the man or woman carrying the spear or the rifle and marching or riding into battle was the warrior, as were their opponents; now, things are considerably less clear-cut.

The infantry Marine or Soldier marching out on a foot patrol is certainly a warrior, as is the supply officer leading a logistics convoy through a contested area of desert. But what about the staff officer who never leaves the relative safety and comfort of a large FOB? Are "fobbits" warriors? What about members of the armed forces who have never deployed? And what about insurgents, fighting either for causes we support, or fighting against us?

As noted before, Pressfield intimates that perhaps everyone is a warrior; on the back cover of his book, he writes: "We are all warriors. Each of us struggles every day..." Sorry, Mr. Pressfield, but not everyone is a warrior. It takes more than a bit of an internal struggle to claim this word with any sort of authority. According to the Oxford and Cambridge dictionaries, a warrior is:

> A brave or experienced soldier or fighter; a person who has experience and skill in fighting, esp. as a soldier.

By this definition, we see that not even all members of the U.S. military can truly claim this sobriquet; but in this day and age where both East and West appear to follow a philosophy of "every corpse a hero or a martyr" perhaps every member of the military profession may reasonably take up the title of warrior, be their exposure to risk ever so slight.

I submit that any man or woman who takes up arms in the service of their country, or of a cause in which they believe may rightly be called a warrior, and both they and their cause or country would benefit if they adopted a Warrior Ethos suited to the modern world and the future.

I won't attempt to make subjective judgments about the justice of the reason which impels these warriors to fight, nor will I judge them less than warriors if their contribution to the cause takes place completely off the kinetic battlefield.

So, for the purpose of this short book, the warrior is simply a person who is willing to subordinate themselves to the demands of a country or a cause, and is willing to aid other members of their organization to engage in violence, and to kill or die or risk severe injury themselves to advance the interests of that country or cause.

Having defined that key term, we can now go on to address each of Pressfield's questions.

1. Does a ~~fighting man~~ fighter require a flag or a cause to claim a code of honor? Or does a Warrior Ethos arise spontaneously, called forth by necessity and the needs of the human heart? Is honor coded into our genes?

First off, let's dispense with that misogynistic term "fighting man". Then let's address the other problem with this question, which is that Pressfield has conflated a "code of honor" with a "warrior ethos" – the former may be part of the latter, but not necessarily; they are certainly not the same thing.

And I reach the same conclusion as Pressfield, on the first count. A flag is not required, but something is; family, tribe, team. Honor only has a context when framed in terms of a group, not when viewed through a solely individual lens. For this reason, Mafia dons, feuding West Virginia backwoodsmen, and Pashtun insurgents can all claim, with complete honesty, that they follow a code of honor, although liberal Western societies, to include the military members of those societies tend not to agree with these particular sorts of "honor codes".

As for any Warrior Ethos, it cannot emerge spontaneously, but must be developed, nurtured, and molded. The nature of the resultant ethos will be very much determined by the nature of the training that develops it, and particularly by the example set by the presumably older, wiser mentors who are helping to inculcate it in a younger generation of warriors.

But is honor coded into our genes? Here to I am in agreement with Pressfield, though I reach my conclusion somewhat more scientifically. There is a whole field of research called Behavioral Genetics; and it turns out that some things *are* in fact genetically coded. Aspects such as temperament, personality, intelligence, and appetite all have a genetic component, but that is not true of the abstract aspects of human nature such as honor, piety, virtue, and honesty.

If such things are not genetically predetermined, then they must be learned attributes that manifest themselves through a person's behaviors; and here my perspective diverges sharply from Pressfield's.

He believes that warriors (and people in general) must be shamed into overcoming physiologically hard-wired reactions like fear. In fact, for Pressfield "the opposite of shame is honor." Untrue.

The two words are not antonyms: according to the Merriam-Webster dictionary, shame is a painful emotion caused by consciousness of guilt, shortcoming, or impropriety; something that brings censure or reproach, or something to be regretted. Honor, on the other hand, is defined as public esteem; reputation; chastity, integrity, and civility.

In Pressfield's analysis, shame is the stick by which people are to be conditioned; honor and love are to be the carrots. Pressfield gives an example of Alexander the Great attempting to shame his men into continuing their campaign in India by showing off his own war wounds, a classic case of cherry-picking the facts of history. In that early instance, the trick worked, but eventually, the threat of mutiny could no longer be forestalled by such tactics, and Alexander was obliged to retreat from India in 326 BC.

This shows the limitations of shame and bullying by high-ranking officers and NCOs in getting their troops to overcome their fears and behave correctly. Something more is needed; I would suggest that it is the "Five E's" of experience, empathy, example, education and empowerment.

Experience is the ability to look a person in the eye and tell them honestly that you are asking nothing of them that you haven't done yourself when you ordering them into action; and also, the ability to speak with the same honesty about mistakes that you've made in the past, to prevent them from making those same mistakes in the future.

Empathy is the ability to put yourself in someone else's shoes – and having experience makes it easier to do that.

Example - there is no better way to inspire performance than to set a sterling example each and every day. A leader must come in earlier and leave later than their troops; must set the standard for appearance, physical and mental preparation, and job performance. They must ensure that their troops have been fed and paid and mentored before worrying about themselves.

Education - Troops at every level should be educated through formal and informal programs. The military is good at setting education goals; we are not as good at ensuring our folks achieve them. The Commandant publishes his Reading List; there is no mechanism to ensure that Marines are making steady progress through it.

Special courses have been set up to educate junior leaders at the rank of Corporal – often, class seats go unfilled because those Marines were "needed at the office." Language and cultural training, professional reading, college courses, military-specific courses, and technical training are all aspects of education in which every warrior should be seeking continual improvement.

Education is physical as well as mental; 3000 repetitions of a martial arts move is required to make it second nature; again, we are better at creating excellent programs than ensuring that our troops have the time and motivation to advance through them. This must change.

Empowerment; last but certainly not least, the warrior who has benefited from the experience, empathy, and example of their leaders, and from the opportunity to advance their education should be empowered to lead others, to suggest improvements to existing processes, to accomplish the mission. Good ideas know no rank.

The organization that consistently applies the "Five E's" will find that it doesn't need to rely on using shame to goad its members to "do the right thing" – to act honorably and serve well. Such behavior is the natural result of a command climate that emphasizes education and empowerment, in which leaders at every level display and continually seek to improve the characteristics of experience, empathy, and example.

Under such conditions, we should expect to see a significant reduction in sexual assault, alcohol-related incidents, suicide, and the unique form of bullying known throughout the military as hazing.

2. What does honor consist of—in an age when the concept seems almost abandoned by society at large, at least in the West?

Here it is time to narrow the aperture; it has been said before but it bears repeating – there is no single definition for "honor" that all warrior cultures throughout the world today, or dating back to ancient times would accept.

But if we're going to talk about honor, we need to define it for our own purpose, so here is a definition that would be widely accepted, at least in the Western World.

Honor, for Marines, is considered a "Core Value" – and it comes with a specific definition:

> HONOR: The bedrock of our character. The quality that guides Marines to exemplify the ultimate in ethical and moral behavior; never to lie, cheat, or steal; to abide by an uncompromising code of integrity; to respect human dignity; to have respect and concern for each other. The quality of maturity, dedication, trust, and dependability that commits Marines to act responsibly; to be accountable for actions; to fulfill obligations; and to hold others accountable for their actions.

Unlike earlier honor codes, this one doesn't require us to take an eye for an eye, to commit suicide if we fail to live up to our own code, or if we let down our comrades or superiors. It doesn't compel us to face our enemies in a "fair fight" – in these rather traditional aspects, it is quite forgiving.

This particular definition of honor is, in fact, a good element of a modern warrior ethos, especially when tempered with another characteristic; honesty. A warrior must be honest with, at the very minimum, themselves, and part of that honesty is to acknowledge that honor may not always be the whole answer. This was highlighted in the mandatory ethics training put out by the Commandant and the Sergeant Major of the Marine Corps in 2012.

Part of that training included a variety of escalating scenarios that test the limits of honorable behavior. "Would you steal?" Everyone answers no. "Would you steal food to keep yourself from starving?" Some answer yes – others have to think a while before answering in the negative. "Would you steal food to keep your child from starving?" Now the pendulum tilts. Hands go up. A room full of officers reveals their true natures. Does this make them dishonorable men and women?

No, it simply shows the limits of the concept of honor.

Lieutenant General Victor "Brute" Krulak, USMC, (Retired) included in *First to Fight: An Inside View of the U.S. Marine Corps* a whole chapter entitled "The Honorable Art of Institutional Theft," which began as follows:

> Military units have stolen from one another throughout history, but the Marines have probably brought institutional theft to a higher state of development than anyone else. Partly because of the exhilaration of the chase, but far more because of poverty, the Marines— particularly those of the 1920s and 1930s— strove to outwit and steal from one another and from others, just to make the supply books balance.

He acknowledged a few rules;

> You stole for the outfit, never for yourself. You didn't steal weapons. Some poor fellow was signed up for every one. And, if you knew what was good for you, you didn't steal from the Quartermaster.

Everything from jeeps to toilet paper, food to tents was stolen with a certain sense of pride; there is even an entire building (Building 131 on Camp Pendleton) that was created entirely of stolen materials. Lieutenant General Krulak explained that,

While theft, institutional or otherwise, is on its face mischievous and wicked, it is not hard to see how it became a way of Marine Corps life given the dedication to making do with very little that, of necessity, had pervaded the Corps for so long. Alas, it is sadly true that just as much of America has evolved, over the past generation, into an Oliver Twist society, holding out its bowl and saying, "Please, sir, some more," so has the Marine Corps in some respects strayed from its frugal ways of 1800 to 1940.

The lesson here is that there are few absolutes where notions of what is honorable are concerned; what would get you a court-martial today has gotten past warriors accolades from their superiors. Honor may be a good start, but a well-constructed Warrior Ethos needs considerably more.

3. What is the Warrior Ethos? Where did it come from? What form does it take today?

Ethos is a word of ancient Greek origin, which is used to describe the guiding beliefs or ideals that characterize a group, a nation, or an ideology. It is not to be confused with ethics; according to the Metropolitan John of Pergamon, one of the heads of the Orthodox Church:

There is a strong distinction between ethos and ethics, in that ethos is applied within a culture and presupposes community, whereas ethics operate on the basis of principles and are rooted in systems of thought.

In other words, ethics are something that you have internalized; an ethos is something that you adopt based on your culture and the company you keep. In *The Warrior's Honor*, Michael Ignatieff writes of "the codes of a warrior's honor."

While these codes vary from culture to culture, they seem to exist in all cultures, and their common features are among the oldest artifacts of human morality... As ethical systems, they were primarily concerned with establishing the rules of combat and defining the system of moral etiquette by which warriors judged themselves to be worthy of mutual respect.

He cautions, however, that:

Warrior codes were sharply particularist: that is, they applied only to certain people, not to others. The protections afforded by the chivalric code applied only to Christians. Toward infidels, a warrior could behave without restraint.

Which leads us to Pressfield's final question:

4. Do we fight by a code? If so, what is it?

This is simple. Yes, most warriors fight by a code of some sort; these days, that code is generally called, in the West, the "Rules of Engagement" colloquially known as the ROE.

For NATO forces, these rules are generally based on international law, although their interpretation in our latest wars in Iraq and Afghanistan should raise serious questions for all warriors, especially in such areas as the use of drones, signature strikes based on "patterns of life," and other tactical aspects. Most other countries who are signatories to the Geneva and Hague Conventions (known as the Laws of Armed Conflict) are likely to fight by a similar ROE.

Other modern-day warriors fighting for non-state actors have quite different codes, ranging from the simple eye-for-an-eye retribution often seen in the Syrian Civil War, to the Taliban's *Laheya*, or code of conduct, most recently updated in 2010, that contains 15 chapters defining how its members should conduct themselves in their conflict with their opponents.

The existence of a code for warriors to tell them when and how they may legitimately engage in lethal violence is not new; it is, however, probably poorly understood especially at the lowest levels of most military forces, and there is a lack of a good mechanism for individual warriors to question the legitimacy of either the road to war or actions in that war. Similarly, it is sometimes either misunderstood or ill-applied by officers at the highest ranks, and the lines are further blurred when civilian agencies are allowed to use lethal force, such as in the CIA's drone program.

Can a Warrior Ethos support a war that, judged fairly on the long-established principles of *jus ad bellum* (the right choice to go to war) is not just? Or that is waged with tactics that violate the Laws of Armed Conflict? And if not, how can a modern warrior avoid fighting in such a war without penalty?

Since Nuremberg, it has been tacitly understood that "We were just following orders" is no justification for warriors to commit crimes in and of war; but fifty years later, warriors still appear to be following orders of questionable legitimacy just as obediently as earlier generations did.

Part of the issue is that beyond a Warrior Ethos, there is a need to revise the very structure of our modern militaries, and of the international system that employs war as a natural extension of diplomacy.

For non-state actors such as rebel forces, there is not currently a standard political mechanism for them to obtain redress for their grievances short of fighting insurgencies against the governments they view as corrupt, or foreign forces which they view as occupiers.

For members of national military forces, there is similarly no mechanism for them to "opt out" of a particular war on the basis that it is unjust, or to eschew the employment of particular weapons systems or tactics that they judge to be unfair to their opponent, without being forced to either give up their profession entirely, or perhaps being subject to incarceration or even execution.

Thus, while a Warrior Ethos will be of some benefit, it is not all that is required by this generation of ethical warriors, or the next. Significant structural changes in national and international norms are also needed, but that is beyond the scope of this book, which is written to propose an ethos to help modern warriors deal with the way the world is, rather than the way it could, and perhaps should be.

Therefore, having answered Pressfield's questions, let me now address the form and function of a modern Warrior Ethos, and bring this counterpoint to a close.

First, our Warrior Ethos is for warriors; while the ordinary citizen might find it a useful resource, we don't imagine that it is either designed or suitable for everyone.

Our Warrior Ethos gives short shrift to the historical concepts of honor; we recognize a limited degree of value in the mental and physical abuse required to mold men and women with shame and bullying. Instead, our definition of honor is similar to the current Marine Corps definition; grounded on the principles of integrity and a respect for human dignity, it exalts the admirable qualities of maturity, dedication, trust, and dependability that guides us to act responsibly, fulfill our obligations, to be accountable for our own actions and to hold our fellow warriors accountable for theirs.

In the context of this ethos, leaders at all levels strive to employ the "Five E's" of experience, empathy, example, education and empowerment, creating a command climate that emphasizes education and empowerment for all members, and in which leaders set the example and continually seek to make decisions based on empathy and experience.

In adopting this approach, we set ourselves to the difficult task of creating tough, realistic, standards-based training and using it to forge young men and women into tools of the State in a manner that is both respectful of their humanity, and inculcates a fundamental respect for *all* people, even those against whom they are obliged to fight.

Encapsulated, our mantra might sound similar to General James "Mad Dog" Mattis' famous dictum for his Marines – "No better friend, no worse enemy."

But let's consider what is implicit in Mattis' aphorism, which he borrowed, it should be noted, from the Roman dictator, Lucius Cornelius Sulla. One expects that a military opponent will attempt to kill us in hot-blooded combat. But let's consider what a "worse" enemy might do.

For starters, a worse enemy might prey upon members of his or her own unit, or upon themselves. Statistically, a Marine today is far more likely to be sexually assaulted by another

Marine than by an enemy soldier; and is more likely to kill themselves than to die fighting on the battlefield. Today, we are in fact our own worst enemies.

To continue, though, a worse enemy might not just kill us, they might also kill our families and known associates to discourage other would-be fighters. A worse enemy might torture prisoners in an attempt to discover our plans. A worse enemy would not scruple to execute in cold blood prisoners who were a burden, represented a threat, or simply aroused anger or disgust. We do not want our adversaries to be unable to imagine a more horrific opponent when they think of us; and we certainly do not want our fellow service members to, either.

Instead, we'd like potential opponents to think of us as "No better friend, no better enemy." They should be convinced that we can be trusted to deal fairly before and after combat operations, and to operate scrupulously within the letter of international law while engaged in fighting.

They should know that we will only fight in just wars, that we will never be dragged to a level where we allow ourselves to inflict civilian casualties as a means of limiting our own, and that we will fairly and transparently prosecute those members of our forces who commit atrocities.

And our fellow service members should expect that they can trust the man and woman to their left and right implicitly, secure in the knowledge that a shared ethos shields them from potential misconduct, and that breaches of that trust will be swiftly dealt with in a fair and transparent manner, regardless of rank, gender, or any other factor.

Sadly, it appears that there is still great truth in the quote by the philosopher George Santayana, "Only the dead have seen the end of war." Since the dawn of warfare, about 5000 years ago, the human race has been faced with a challenge as to how to comport themselves in violent conflict, and many different approaches have been tried.

For thousands of years, to loot and rape was part of a warrior's reward for succeeding in battle; to take enemy prisoners or civilians as slaves, or to put whole populations to death was not uncommon. It is from this historical epoch that many of Pressfield's examples come.

The rise of Hindu, Jewish, Christian, and Muslim faiths marked a turning point for military behaviors in much of the world; in principle, at least, warriors were supposed to act with restraint, rather than applying the mantra of "all's fair in love and war".

In India, the *Mahabharata*, one of the great Sanskrit epics, outlined some basic boundaries; chariots should only attack other chariots, no poisoned or barbed arrows should be used, armies should fight for conquest, not out of anger, and wounded men should be treated fairly.

The Old Testament required the Israelites to offer peace before besieging an opposing city, and the first Muslim Caliph, Abu Bakr instructed his men that they must not commit treachery, not mutilate dead bodies, and not kill old men, women or children.

But the historical record shows that these early attempts to regulate the bloody business of war fell far short of the desired result. It would take another 1500 years marked by Crusades, Mongol invasions, religious wars throughout Europe, and early colonial adventures in Asia, Africa, and the Americas for institutions such as slavery to be abolished and warfare to be more thoroughly reined in.

European leaders agreed that wars were to be limited to achieving the political goals that started the conflict, and should be ended quickly, avoiding unnecessary destruction. Non-combatants were to be protected, and the rights of prisoners respected. Peace was to be restored as quickly as possible. Despite the fact that these frameworks failed to prevent the deaths of millions in two World Wars, or the unleashing of atomic weaponry, with each successive generation, advances *are* made in regulating the conduct of war.

Many nations have signed up to ban cluster bombs and landmines; a move is now afoot to regulate "killer robots" – which may sound like something out of a science fiction movie, but can in fact be easily manufactured with today's modern technology.

There are still many challenges, as evidenced by on-going conflicts around the world, but there is reason to hope that as the 21st Century continues, modern militaries can transition to organizations whose missions are summed up by the current U.S. Navy slogan "A Global Force for Good."

Responses to recent disasters, from the 2004 Asian Tsunami to the 2010 earthquake in Haiti have shown that military forces can have huge positive impacts in a time of crisis, while missions like "Pacific Partnership" reinforce the idea that preventative medicine, construction, and confidence-building between nations can help improve the world in which we live.

The Warrior Ethos which I have laid out here is one that should provide a suitable guide for all ranks when considering how to act in both conflict and disaster response.

Junior troops cannot go wrong by undertaking the completion of tough, realistic, standards-based training under the keen eye of their superiors, and then conducting themselves both on and off-duty in a manner that demonstrates a fundamental respect for *all* people, even those against whom they are obliged to fight, and especially toward their countrymen and women who serve side-by-side in uniform.

Senior warriors, who have benefited from such initial training, who have developed their own extensive experience while using those same tools of empathy, education, and empowerment, and who have served with honor in difficult situations along the full spectrum of civil-military operations will certainly feel themselves obliged to work to ensure that future conflicts are based on justice, not expediency; that tactics and operations are in keeping with the principles of *jus in bello* (proper conduct of war).

Some great men and women, like George Washington, Dwight D. Eisenhower, John McCain, Colin Powell, and Tammy Duckworth before them, will make the transition from warriors to politicians or diplomats and play a vital role in the design of new national and international mechanisms for preventing civil wars, insurgencies, and inter-state war.

A few may even go so far as to challenge the very nature of an international system that employs war as a natural extension of diplomacy, following the example of two-time Medal of Honor winner Major General Smedley Butler, USMC, (Retired) who suggested that military forces be confined by law to the territorial lands and waters of their own countries, and that wars should be entered into only if those eligible to fight voted to do so.

Finally, all warriors will benefit from fighting an enemy who knows that combat is a last resort; that on our side it will be hard-fought, but always within the laws of war, and that we will never inflict civilian casualties as a means of limiting our own.

Our enemy must know that if taken prisoner, they will be accorded their rights under international law and that if any member of our forces commits an atrocity, they will be prosecuted with fairness and transparency. And our Nation must know that it can entrust its sons and daughters to our ranks; not to be broken down with shame, not to pumped up to "avenge every insult", and not to suffer from high rates of sexual assault and suicide, but to be tested and tempered in the forges of our basic training curriculums with firmness, fairness and dignity, and to be led always by officers and NCOs who use the tools of empathy, education, and empowerment to set an example worthy of our enlightened age, so that whether a modern warrior serves four years or 30, that they return to civil life having grown as a person and having developed their abilities to lead, to follow, and to work as a member of a team.

CONCLUSION

Pressfield is right to say that service as a warrior is not the be-all and end-all of life. None of us are born warriors; relatively few of us will die as warriors. For most, it is a stage of life that lasts as little as four years, as much as 30 years, but a stage that has great power to shape us, for better or worse.

So let us be, as Pressfield says, warriors of the heart;

> ... and enlist in our inner cause the virtues we have acquired through blood and sweat in the sphere of conflict— courage, patience, selflessness, loyalty, fidelity, self-command, respect for elders, love of our comrades (and of the enemy), perseverance, cheerfulness in adversity and a sense of humor, however terse or dark.

But let us not be shamed or bullied into displaying these virtues, nor be misled into thinking that a Bronze Age version of honor is suitable for the Information Age warrior.

Instead, let us be molded into warriors by older, wiser men and women who treat us with firmness, fairness, and dignity; leaders with experience and empathy who set the example, who educate and empower us so that, as we rise through the ranks of our warrior societies, we can in turn develop those same principles in the generation of future warriors who will follow in *our* footsteps.

If we do these things, we may walk always with head held high, knowing that we are a force to be reckoned with in wartime, and ambassadors of goodwill at all times; that it can be truly said that in each of us you will find "No better friend, no better enemy."

BIBLIOGRAPHY

This book has been informed in large part by my interpretation of Steven Pressfield's 2011 book *The Warrior Ethos*, and references the following additional sources:

The Old Testament

The Bhagavad-Gita

The Mahabharata

Histories, Herodotus

The Life of Lycurgus, Plutarch

The Peloponnesian War, Thucydides

The Warrior's Honor, Michael Ignatieff

Honor: A History, James Bowman

First to Fight: An Inside View of the U.S. Marine Corps, Lieutenant General Victor "Brute" Krulak, USMC, (Retired)

Six Weeks: The Short and Gallant Life of the British Officer in the First World War, John Lewis-Stempel

Bloody Red Tabs: General Officer Casualties of the Great War, 1914-1918, Frank Davies and Graham Maddocks

War is a Racket, Major General Smedley D. Butler, USMC (Retired)

On Killing, Lieutenant Colonel Dave Grossman, USA

Achilles in Vietnam, Jonathan Shay, M.D., PhD

The Face of Battle, John Keegan

Man and His Symbols, Carl Gustav Jung

King, Warrior, Magician, Lover: Rediscovering the Archetypes of the Mature Masculine, Robert L. Moore and Douglas Gillette

The Fog of War, Errol Morris

Lucius Cornelius Sulla

Diodorus Siculus

Sir Arthur "Bomber" Harris, RAF

General Curtis LeMay, USAF

General James "Mad Dog" Mattis, USMC

The Honorable Mr. Robert McNamara as quoted in *The Fog of War*

Robert Woosnam-Savage, as quoted in *TIME Magazine*

Colonel Tu

Abu Bakr

Carl Gustav Jung

Metropolitan John of Pergamon

Baz Luhrmann

Mary Schmich

Santayana

EDWARD H. CARPENTER is the author of *Seven Lives to Repay Our Country, Ho B-52,* and *Lethargica*, and he has written for the *Marine Corps Gazette* and *Current Intelligence.* Formerly an Army enlisted man, he has served for over 15 years as an officer of Marines, from Indonesia to Saudi Arabia, Japan to Afghanistan, including multiple combat zone deployments. He is unlikely ever to be made an honorary citizen of Sparta.

Made in the USA
Middletown, DE
02 November 2019